I Have Ec

by Althea · pictures by Sarah Altham

Published by Dinosaur Publications

Having eczema is like being covered
from head to toe with an itchy rash.
It is not catching but it is very
irritating.

When it gets very bad
it drives me mad.
I can't help it,
I just have to scratch.
If I scratch too much
it makes my skin bleed
and then it hurts even more,
but I still want to scratch.

I try to remember to press hard on
my skin, which helps to stop the itch.
We file my finger nails very short
to try to stop me hurting myself.

I wear gloves in bed at night.
I wriggle my legs together
to stop the itchiness.

Sometimes, when my eczema
has been very painful,
Dad has bandaged
the worst parts for me.

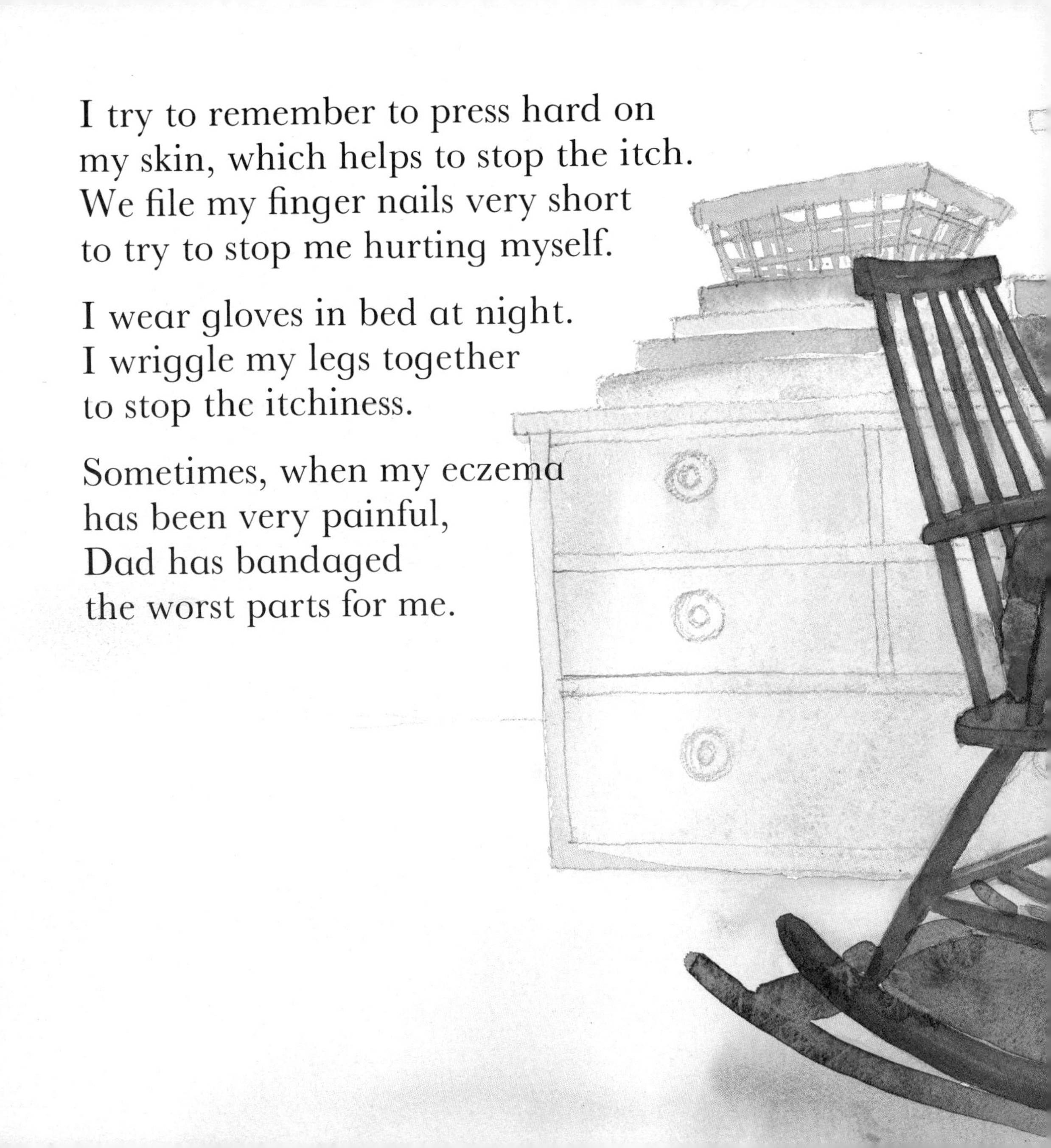

Eczema can get so painful that
it even hurts to smile because
my skin cracks open and bleeds.

I walk around like a penguin
to avoid bending my legs.
It may look funny, but it's no joke.
After sitting it hurts to straighten
my legs again because the skin
cracks open.

When it's really sore like that
I forget that it isn't always as bad
and I feel very sorry for myself.
I forget that most of the time
I can cope, even though it's annoying.

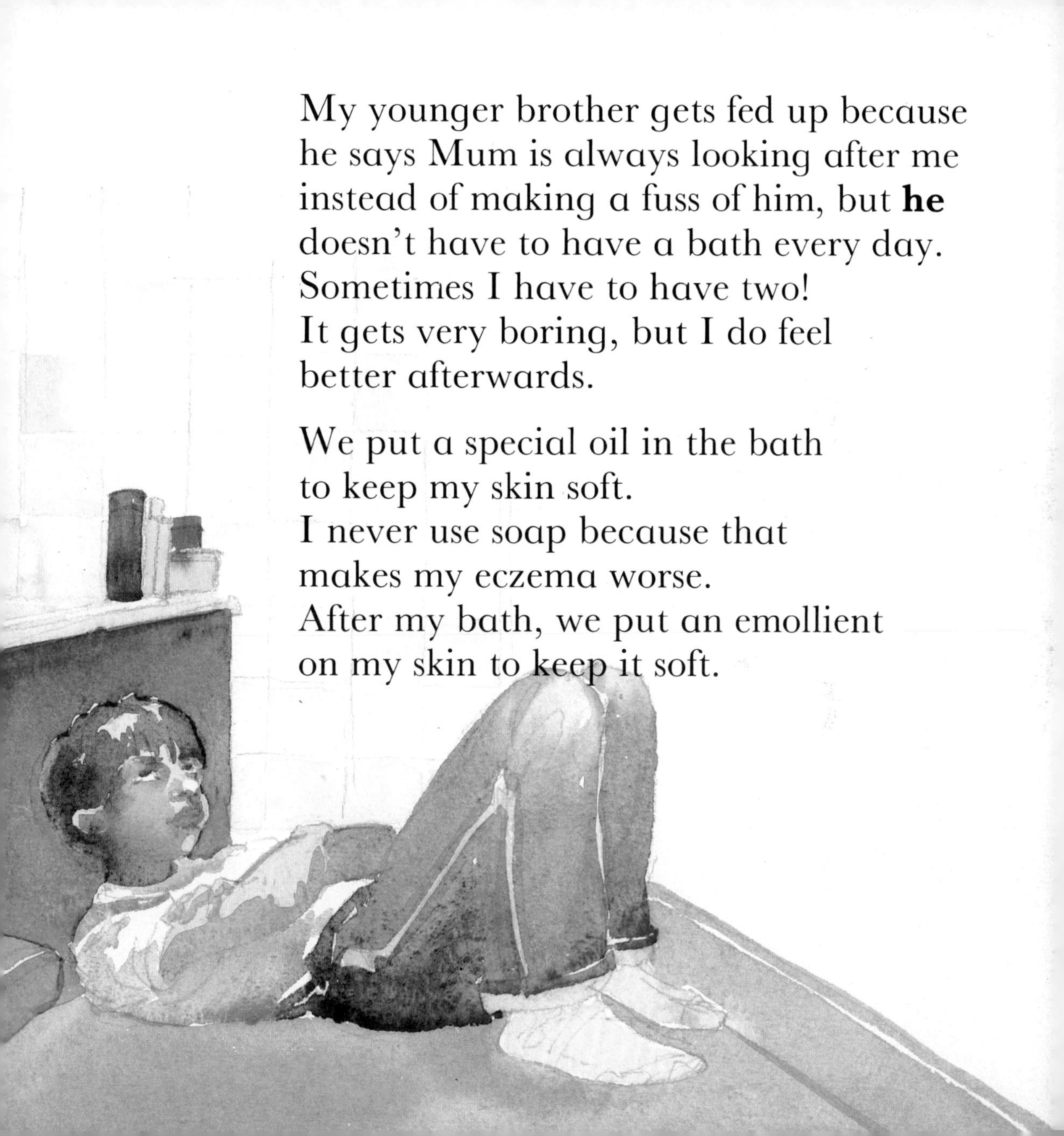

My younger brother gets fed up because he says Mum is always looking after me instead of making a fuss of him, but **he** doesn't have to have a bath every day. Sometimes I have to have two!
It gets very boring, but I do feel better afterwards.

We put a special oil in the bath to keep my skin soft.
I never use soap because that makes my eczema worse.
After my bath, we put an emollient on my skin to keep it soft.

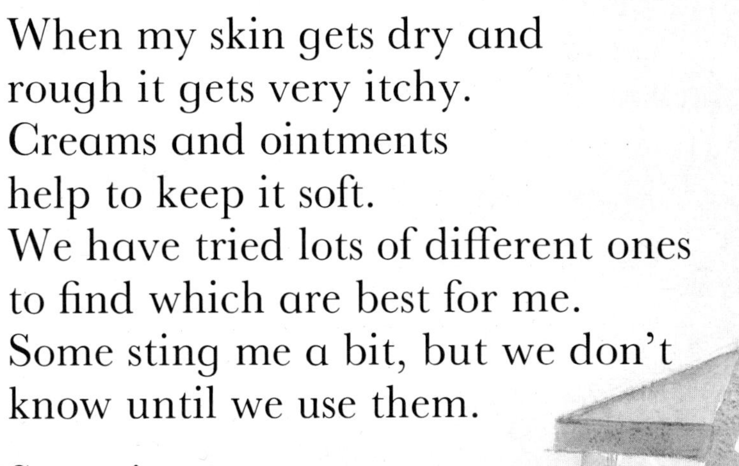

When my skin gets dry and
rough it gets very itchy.
Creams and ointments
help to keep it soft.
We have tried lots of different ones
to find which are best for me.
Some sting me a bit, but we don't
know until we use them.

Sometimes my eczema can get very
bad in places and the skin doctor
has given me steroid ointments
to use when this happens.

When my eczema is bad it can look horrid,
as well as being very painful.
People don't want to touch me.
Sometimes they stare and talk about me
as if I wasn't there!

Other children can be nasty too,
but my friends and my class at school
know that eczema is not catching.

When I wash my hands at school,
I use my cream instead of soap.
I take another cream to school with me
to put on if I start to get itchy, because
the sore rash can start up very suddenly.
My teacher lets me go and get a drink
of cold water, and that seems to help.

When it's very bad I am sometimes
allowed to use the typewriter so
that I don't have to bend my fingers.
It takes me ages to find the letters!

I try not to sit near a radiator
or in the sun because heat makes
my eczema worse. Some of the classrooms
have very big windows which make it
difficult to keep out of the sun.

Some nights when I just can't sleep,
I keep waking Mum and Dad and
we all get very grumpy!
Then it's difficult to wake up
in the morning and I feel tired
at school.

If I get an infection I sometimes
have to take medicine or use special creams.

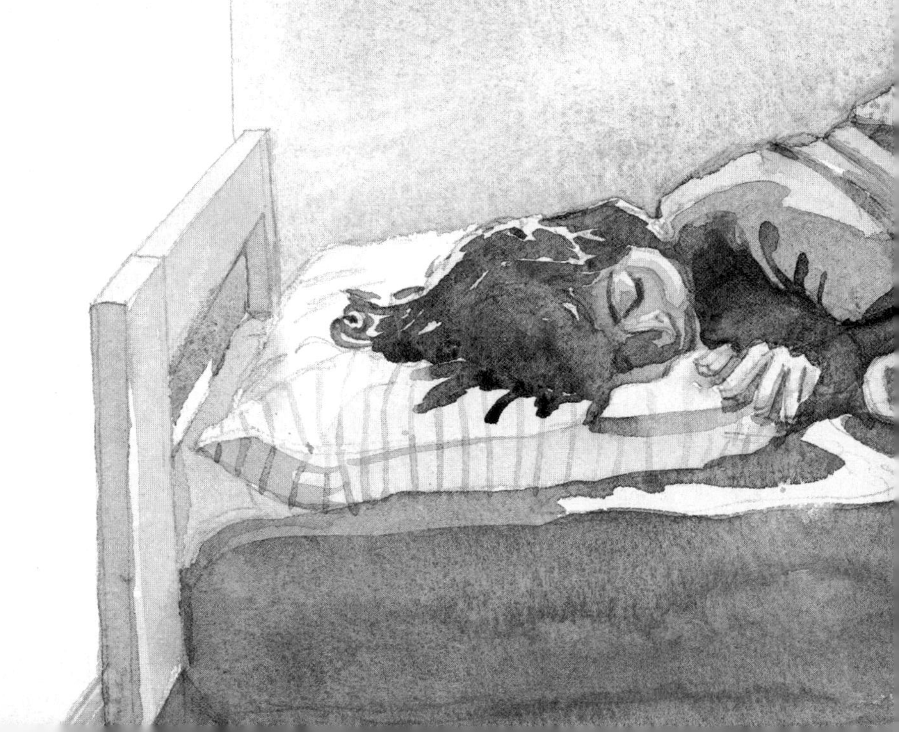

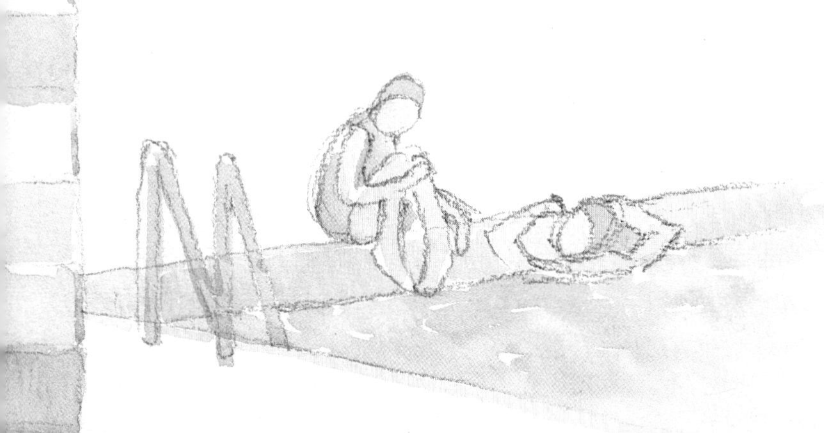

When we go to the swimming pool
I put Vaseline or an emollient
on my skin to protect it before
I swim. Then I have a shower
afterwards to wash off the chlorine.
When I'm dry I put my emollient on again.

My eczema often gets better
when I'm on holiday.
Dad says he feels good too –
it's because we are all
happy and relaxed.

If I forget and play on the carpet
at my friend's house, I know my legs
will be itchy by the time I get home.
They have a cat and the doctor has said
that I might be allergic to cats or dogs.
Some clothes make me itch too, but my
loose cotton clothes are the most comfortable.
Dust seems to make my eczema worse.
Poor Mum complains that she is always
having to clean my room!

Mum is always being given advice!
A friend told her that milk and eggs
sometimes make eczema worse.
I tried giving up milk but it
didn't work for me.
I'm glad because I love cheese.

I don't drink squash or have ice lollies
because we think the colouring
makes my eczema worse.
I have fresh orange juice instead,
and we make our own ice lollies.
They taste much nicer.
Orange juice stings if it gets into
the cracks on my face or fingers,
so I have to be careful when I eat oranges.

Dad used to have eczema
when he was a child,
but he doesn't get it now.
My doctor says that eczema often
clears up as children get older.
Mum says I don't get it as badly
now as I did when I was a baby.